DELPHINIUMS FOR EVERYONE

DELPHINIUMS
for Everyone

STUART OGG, V.M.H.

BLANDFORD PRESS - LONDON

First published 1961

©

Blandford Press Limited
16 West Central Street, London, W.C.1

S/7 70 Y/Y
6/16511 A
639. 9335547.

Printed in Great Britain by Richard Clay and Company Ltd.,
Bungay, Suffolk

CONTENTS

ACKNOWLEDGMENTS

I WISH to acknowledge my grateful thanks to Mr H. G. Witham Fogg for his work on the MS of my book as well as collating some useful information of the past history of the Delphinium; to Mr Alfred Kidney for much invaluable advice and information, and to Miss Vera Frampton for her careful help at all stages. I would also like to thank Mr J. E. Downward, who took the photographs dealing with the propagation by cuttings and division and growing from seed, as well as the plant photographs (Figs 1 to 9).

My special thanks are due to the ladies of the Sevenoaks Flower Club who decorated my home for the benefit of the National Gardens Scheme, demonstrating the usefulness of the Delphinium in the home. The following ladies took part:—Mrs Campbell (Chairman), Mrs Bates, Mrs Linforth, Mrs Potter, Mrs Pugh, Mrs Thompson, and Mrs Vinson.

My final 'thank you' goes to Mr Jeremy McCabe, who took the first-class photographs of the floral arrangements and the individual varieties, both in colour and black and white.

The four fine colour reproductions of the varieties 'Daily Express', 'Mazurka', 'Julia Langdon' and 'Dora Cairncross' were originally photographed by Mr A. C. Hunt for my catalogues.

STUART OGG

LIST OF COLOUR PLATES

LIST OF BLACK AND WHITE ILLUSTRATIONS

Introducing the Delphinium

THE MODERN DELPHINIUM is one of the most beautiful flowers to be found in the garden today. It has often been termed the Queen of the Herbaceous Border, a title which I feel it rightly deserves, even more today than ever before.

It was the ancient Greeks who gave this flower its name, for they saw in the unopened buds of this primitive flower some resemblance to the Dolphin, a likeness which is still preserved in the most modern varieties. At various times and in different countries the delphinium has been known as the King's Spur and the Little Spur, while Larkspur is, of course, the well-known annual. This latter name for describing the family originated in England. The ancient writer Gerard says, that in England 'it is Larkes Spur, larkes heel, larkes toes, larkes clawe and Munkes-hoode'!

There is no difficulty in detecting in the horn-shaped nectary of the flower a resemblance to the spur of a lark's claw.

John Parkinson made several references to the delphinium in his famous *Paradisus Terrestis* of 1640.

There are many excellent species, and some of them are dealt with in Chapter 13. It is regrettable that records of the species used in the raising of the earlier hybrids do not seem to have been preserved. This makes it somewhat difficult to be absolutely sure as to the origin of many of today's strain. One may surmise, if nothing more, that *D. brunonianum* and *D.*

16511A

formosanum were much used, and there can be little doubt that *D. elatum* has brought height into the family.

It is really during the last hundred years or so that the most important and successful work on delphiniums has been carried out in Britain and other countries chiefly by nurserymen, though there have been a number of amateur growers who have had remarkable successes.

It was in 1921 that Mr Watkin Samuel staged his remarkable delphinium exhibit at the Chelsea Flower Show. Nothing approaching the broad-based, pyramidal spikes had ever been seen before, and improvements have continued since that time. Much of the increased popularity of the plant is due to the activities of the Delphinium Society, founded in 1928, although it then had the word 'British' as part of its title.

The 'Bishop' and 'Giant Pacific' strains are now well known, as are the remarkably good varieties raised by Blackmore and Langdon and other specialist growers.

These raisers have worked very hard, and with success, to improve both the range of colours and the constitution of the plant. We now have every shade of blue from the palest to the deepest, and the same with the mauves, from a silvery-mauve to deep purple. There are also combinations of blue and mauve, and purple and blue shades. More recently there have been some white introductions, which came from the United States of America in the first place. While these original plants were not truly perennial, we now have half a dozen or more which will survive our winters, and there is great demand for them.

The same was true of some most beautiful electric-blue varieties which also came from America and which were not perennials originally. Now that they have been grown here for some time and improved, there are some really lovely examples on the market, notably 'Anne Page' and 'Daily Express'.

Such first-class varieties have only come about by the consistent, skilful work of British raisers who have been able to cross the 'Giant Pacific' strain from America with some of the best of the British strains.

You can now obtain plants which have a very wide range of colour with heights ranging from 3 feet to 8 feet with plants that produce spikes from 2 feet to 4 feet in length and with individual pips of from 2 inches to 4 inches in diameter.

Another range of colours which should not be forgotten are the rose and pink shades. The raisers are working very hard to produce some perennial varieties in these shades, but so far I know only of two varieties on the market, and they are not available in very large quantities at the moment. However, I feel that it is only a question of time before we shall have as good a mixture of colours in delphiniums as we possess today in larkspurs.

Many people seem to imagine that to produce delphinium spikes such as are exhibited at the flower shows is a superhuman task. Actually, the modern varieties are no more difficult to grow than the older types, which are seen so frequently growing in gardens. I only wish people would grow some of the better varieties, instead of these very old ones, which only produce very thin spikes of small single flowers. There are excellent varieties these days on the market to suit all pockets.

Besides improving the size and colour of the flowers and the length of the stem, raisers have also lengthened the flowering period. We now have early, mid-season and late varieties, which is a wonderful asset, as it has certainly lengthened the period of display when several sorts are grown.

Although delphiniums can, of course, be planted singly, they always look best in groups of three to five plants. The exact number in the groups will largely depend of course on the width of the herbaceous border.

In the case of a large garden, where there is plenty of room, delphiniums on their own make a fine display, when properly set out. The one disadvantage is that they cannot be followed up with any other plant, and that is why I stress the point of a fair-sized garden for growing them in this way.

The border need not be a very wide one if it is required for delphiniums alone. The only proviso really that is required is to see that the position chosen is a sunny one, and that it does derive some protection from the prevailing winds, though it must not be overhung by trees. There is nothing that I know of that is more disappointing than to have one's best spikes ruined by wind and rain when they are at their best.

◈ 2 ◈

Planting and Cultivation

HOWEVER GOOD the plants themselves may be, unless they are provided with the right soil conditions and suitable surroundings, they will never produce the finest results. Perfect spikes are undoubtedly a reflection of good cultivation, and with the delphinium this means care and forethought. Firstly, we must consider the site. While this must be open and unshaded by overhanging trees, it must not be exposed to winds, for, as I have said, it is very distressing to discover one's choice spikes badly smashed by wind and rain.

If you should decide to plant delphiniums near a hedge, never place them closer than 2 feet to 2 feet 6 inches, preferably farther away, for the roots of hedging subjects always take so much nourishment from the beds and impoverish the soil. It will also be advisable to keep the hedge trimmed back to about 6 feet in height.

I mention these points because I have seen delphiniums 10 to 11 feet high entirely as a result of being grown too close to a very tall hedge. This caused the plants to grow out of all proportion as regards height and quite out of character also.

Delphiniums will grow on most soils which contain lime, but care must be taken as to the best time to plant. Where the soil is naturally very heavy clay, which lies wet and cold during the winter months, it is advisable to plant in the spring, which is generally about the end of February to early March, according to the soil and weather conditions for the particular locality in question.

SOIL PREPARATION

Whenever you decide to plant your delphiniums, the ground must be well prepared and in good condition, for the plants are likely to remain in the same position for some years if properly looked after. Although the plants form a cluster of roots at a shallow depth, they have other roots which go down deeply. This means that the site should be well moved and manured, so that the roots will be able to gain nourishment as needed over a long period. I recently heard of a plant of 'Lady Eleanor' remaining in position for thirty years. This was a record, but it gives some idea of how important it is to prepare your soil well before planting and dig deeply, since the roots continue to go down with age.

So when you have decided on the spot for your delphiniums, see that you work farmyard manure or a good dressing from the mature compost heap well into the soil. If either of these are not available, apply a good dressing of shoddy or meat and bone meal of a fairly coarse grade. These decompose gradually and release their feeding matter over a long period. Dig in the manure or fertiliser, leaving the ground rough until just before planting time. Use a trowel to make the holes, and spread the roots out, working fine soil between and over them.

Proper spacing is necessary, and it is advisable to measure out the ground and place a stake where each plant is to be grown; then rake down the ground finally, and at that stage a dressing (say two ounces to the square yard) of the John Innes base fertiliser, lightly raked in, will prove beneficial. This fertiliser consists of:

2 parts hoof and horn $\frac{1}{8}$ inch grist
2 parts superphosphate of lime
1 part sulphate of potash (parts by weight)

The exact distance between the plants will depend on the space available, but it should never be less than 2 feet each way. Excepting in cold, exposed areas where the soil is inclined to be wet in the winter, plants can be moved from the end of September until the middle of November, taking climatic conditions into consideration. After this period it is better to postpone planting until the middle of February onwards, for it is essential that all plants set out in the autumn should settle down and begin to make some fresh roots before the really cold weather sets in. Otherwise, losses could be very high, especially if the winter should turn wet and cold.

On very heavy clay soil it may never be suitable to plant in the autumn at all, and this can only be determined from your own experience with your local conditions and the advice of your horticultural society or from experienced local gardeners.

One thing that is certain, however, is that if it is possible to plant in the autumn, you do obtain very much better flower spikes the first year than if you have to wait for spring planting.

Whether you plant early or late, should the weather be at all dry in the spring, it is essential to water delphiniums. At that time the plants have to make new roots quickly, in order to support the fresh top growth, and if moisture is lacking, these new shoots are liable to shrivel and die. It must be remembered that it is not until the second season after planting that the spikes are seen at their finest.

One way to secure particularly good spikes in the shortest time is to purchase rooted cuttings during June or early July.

These are either planted straight into their flowering quarters or they may be placed in 6-inch pots, using the John Innes Compost No. 2, and kept in a cold frame until they are well established, when they can be planted out in their flowering quarters during late August or September. By these methods the roots are not disturbed and really good spikes should be produced the next year. For their first season the plants from pots are best restricted to two or three spikes, so that they can build up their strength for the future.

TYING UP

Delphiniums need supporting, but this should be done as inconspicuously as possible.

As soon as the shoots are big enough, your first tie should be carried out straight away, as this first tie acts as a very good sheet anchor. Raffia is often used to make the ties, but I prefer two- or three-ply soft fillis twine. Keep them well tied during the growing period by adding several stakes and ringing the whole plant round in order to allow more freedom of growth.

Several ties will be necessary, according to the size of the spike, but never make these too tight, otherwise the spikes may break off just at the base.

FEEDING AND WATERING

However well prepared and enriched the soil may have been prior to planting, some additional feeding will be necessary. Bone meal is one of the best and safest foods for delphiniums, and if it is dusted on the soil around the plants, each spring, it will lead to the building up of really healthy growth. Its feeding properties are gradually released in such a way that the roots can use exactly what they need without overfeeding or the production of too lush a growth. An annual dressing of bone

16

PLATE I A fine spike of 'Purple Prince'
PLATE II Two spikes of 'Destiny'

PLATE III Arrangement of delphinium 'Sonata', *Alstroemaria Ligtu* hybrids and annual chrysanthemum, with *prunus pissardii*

PLATE IV Arrangement of delphinium 'Audrey Mott', pale pink carnations, and 'Esther Read', dyed the same colour

meal ensures that the roots will be able to support first-class spikes.

I am often asked what I feed my delphiniums on, because they are grown in what one might term a sand-pit. When the plants are about a foot high they are given a feed of dried blood, which is watered in, unless a good rain follows its application. As soon as the flower spikes begin to form, the plants are given a pinch of sulphate of potash. This too is watered in, and not only helps to counteract any soft growth but firms up the stems, and also helps to bring out the colour.

If when growth reaches 2 to $2\frac{1}{2}$ feet high it is possible to mulch your plants with good cow manure, there will be no need to feed with dried blood, although the sulphate of potash should still be given.

Watering plays an important part in the growing of delphiniums. Particularly during the flowering period, they must never be allowed to become too dry, for this only shortens the season of flowering. When water is applied, it should be given in generous quantities and not in frequent sprinklings, which would tend to bring the roots to the surface.

Unless seed is required to be saved, remove the flower spikes as soon as they pass out of colour, but keep on watering the plants as necessary, for this will build up the crowns for another season. Sufficient root moisture will also encourage the current secondary growths to produce quite a good second crop of flowers, which, though not so robust as the first spikes, are nevertheless a very welcome sight.

SEASONAL SETBACKS

Climatic conditions have a greater influence on growth than we perhaps realise. For example, if we have a mild autumn which is carried on into January, this encourages the new season's growth to develop too quickly. When severe weather follows, as it nearly always does, the young shoots are cut down by frost. We experienced this very badly in the spring of 1958, when we had some varieties completely cut down by the frost, resulting in the spikes subsequently produced being poorer in every respect. Some plants showed the effects of frost in a different way. They produced flower spikes which were leggy, having far too big a gap between the last batch of leaves and the first florets.

Sometimes, as the result of bad checks through drought and cold winds, the plants become hard, and growth is slow. Then in sheer desperation one is inclined to overfeed the plants, but this only leads to the spikes becoming malformed or fasciated.

Sometimes flat stems, thickly matted with florets, will develop, and usually they snap off before their colour is seen. This is another seasonal happening, and many growers may never be troubled with it at all.

So do not get too worried, as in most cases these setbacks are generally seasonal. With good soil, careful feeding and judicious watering during dry weather, there is little likelihood of disappointment, and the dangers from these climatic conditions can be avoided, or at any rate lessened.

MULCHING

I have already referred to mulching with manure as a means of providing extra feeding. While I prefer to use good rotted cow manure as a mulch, town dwellers will not have ready access to this. There are other materials that can be used for this purpose. Apart from mature compost, granulated peat and straw are excellent; not that they provide feeding matter, but because they prevent the surface soil from drying out, which means that the plants will not be checked because of drought. These two must not be regarded as a substitute for the feeding previously outlined, but as something additional. I would not especially recommend grass mowings, as these may tend to heat.

THINNING

Once established, delphiniums will usually produce many basal shoots, and unless the number is reduced, the quality of the spike will be affected. Where border adornment is the only object, all of the strongest shoots may be allowed to develop, which will lead to a massed effect rather than the production of exhibition spikes. Certainly for the first season, I would cut out the weakest shoots, leaving two or three to each plant, which should give quite a good result. In subsequent seasons most plants should be able to carry five or six first-class spikes. In order to achieve this, all the remaining shoots above this number should be cut out. It is very tempting to leave many more on, but the more shoots that are left, the weaker will be the spikes and the smaller the florets.

WINDBREAKS

While it is never wise to grow delphiniums too near a hedge, it is always an asset if such a barrier is available, or if one can be planted. Where this is not possible, or where one has to wait until a hedge is tall enough to act as a windbreak, there are alternative ways of providing protection from winds. Wattle fencing, for example, can be quite artistic and is less formal than a boarded fence or wall. Then there is the material used so effectively for protecting hop gardens from prevailing winds. This consists of fine-meshed canvas netting, which must be very firmly fastened to strong posts. All such means of protection should be in position before the plants are too tall. Even before they are fully developed, the flower spikes become heavy, especially in wet weather, and might become severely damaged if blown down.

Once the main spikes lose their colour they can be cut down. Such action will encourage the side spikes (laterals) to develop, and their flowers, although smaller, will help to prolong the display. Often when these main stems have entirely finished their growth and are cut down one or two of the later basal shoots will delight us with a further show of bloom, going on into September.

❧ 3 ❧

The Two Main Types

∽∽∽∽∽∽∽∽∽∽∽∽∽∽∽∽∽∽∽∽∽∽∽∽

WHILE IT IS CERTAIN that the modern delphinium owes its origin to the fusion of the qualities of many species, coming from various parts of the world, there is no detailed record available. The majority of the species are greatly inferior to the lovely plants we are now accustomed to see, but some of course have individual grace and charm which makes them worth growing.

There is little, if any, doubt that the two species which have had most influence in giving us the present-day delphinium are *D. elatum* and *D. belladonna*. Nearly all the largest-flowered varieties are known under the group name of elatum because they resemble *D. elatum* in shape and habit. Occasionally they are referred to as the hollyhock type because of the shape and size of the florets, and this is certainly the section in which there is the greatest range of varieties.

It is from this section that we have the extremely large number of blue shades. There is no other flower that possesses so many colour tones, and while it is not unusual to hear a colour described as 'delphinium blue' it would be very difficult indeed to fix a particular shade under this heading. There is, in fact, a great divergence of opinion as to what constitutes a delphinium blue, since the colour of the flower varies from a pale Cambridge blue to a dark Oxford blue.

It is always a help to have the varieties of any flower group under colour headings, more especially so when one may be seeking a particular shade. The following list is given as a good cross section of the main varieties in all shades. Each one has proved itself to be reliable under varying cultural conditions.

PALE BLUE. Lady Eleanor, Oenone Lang, Flora Campbell, Anona, Sea Mist, Sonata, Audrey Mott and Horizon.

LIGHT BLUE WITH BLACK EYE. Daily Express, Chas. F. Langdon, Blue Beauty, Etonian, Dame Myra Curtis, Nora O'Fallon and Romance.

LIGHT BLUE AND MAUVE. Mazurka, Oberon, Titania, Jennifer Langdon.

MID-BLUE. Isla, Marion, Mermaid, Destiny, Conquest, Maid of Bath, Moon Rocket.

GENTIAN-BLUE. Anne Page, Lady Wightman, Valentia, Lorna, Charon, Ivy Ridgewell.

DEEP BLUE. Eva Gower, Royalist, Duchess of Portland, Supreme, Neptune, Côte d'Azur, Gladys Sharp, Royal Marine, Jack Tar.

LIGHT MAUVE. Bee Elliott, Olivia, Silver Moon, Bridesmaid, Margaret Farrand, Melora, Great Britain.

DEEP MAUVE. Porthos, Twertonian, Cinderella, Julia Langdon, Judy Knight.

DEEP MAUVE AND BLUE. W. B. Cranfield.

DEEP PURPLE AND BLUE. Dora Cairncross, Peacock, Fred Yule, Purple Ruffles, Kent Messenger.

PURPLE. Purple Prince, Mogul, Guy Langdon, Purple Triumph, Minerva, Wessex.

WHITE. Swan Lake, Janice, Everest, Charles Neaves.

PINK. Tilly Knight.

Delphinium belladonna is quite distinct, and although less popular than the elatum type, all the present-day named varieties are lovely. They are less tall and very compact, with well-branched spikes with deeply cut leaves, presenting a light, graceful appearance. They are rather easier to grow than the tall section and in many cases are constitutionally stronger. The belladonnas are excellent as cut flowers either used by themselves or in mixed arrangements, when they give that extra lightness and gracefulness so often needed.

There are only a few named varieties available, and the following are among the very best, growing 3 to 4 feet in height.

LIGHT BLUE. Blue Bees, Capri, Fernleigh Beauty.
BRIGHT BLUE. Azure Queen, Naples.
GENTIAN-BLUE. Bonita.
BLUE AND MAUVE. Wendy.
DARK BLUE. Lamartine.
WHITE. Moerheimii.
PINK. Pink Sensation.

'Pink Sensation' is usually classed under the belladonna varieties, since it is of similar habit. It came, however, from a chance seedling in a Dutch nursery and is sometimes listed as *D. X ruysii*. It is usually about 3 feet high and has dark glossy leaves with rather dull, though quite pleasing, rose and pink flowers of slightly drooping habit.

❧ 4 ❧

Delphinium Borders

〜〜〜〜〜〜〜〜〜〜〜〜〜〜〜〜〜〜〜〜〜〜〜〜〜〜〜

WHILE IT IS MORE USUAL to arrange and plant a border consisting of many different types of plants, varying in habit as well as colour, the specialised border is becoming more popular. Such borders may be planned for foliage effect, for scent, to attract bees or to provide colour at a particular time of the year. It is perhaps not very often that one finds a border devoted entirely to delphiniums. There is no reason why such borders should not be planned on exactly the same lines as a dahlia border.

In this case the tall varieties are placed at the back, with the medium and dwarf sorts being grown in front. This gives rather a formal effect, and it is often better to bring some of the medium-growing varieties towards the front. This means that one is able to see the full beauty of all the spikes, some of which would otherwise be partly hidden by the plants in front.

The planning of a border which is to be devoted entirely to growing delphiniums needs quite a lot of thought, as there are several points to be considered, such as the colour of the background and position in the garden generally. I personally prefer to group my varieties in blocks of five, ten or even fifteen plants of one variety, depending a great deal on the width of the border. I feel that bold blocks of one variety give a greater colour effect, especially at a distance, than the placing of smaller blocks of several varieties.

FIG 1—Division of the old root by using a sharp knife.

FIG 2—A plant before the cuttings are taken off.

FIG 3—Top two cuttings show the firm base before removing foliage, and the bottom three cuttings are trimmed for insertion into box or pot.

FIG 4—Insertion into box with fingers either side to firm the cutting. Note that the cuttings shown are poor examples, having been photographed late in the season.

Fig 5—Rooted cuttings early in the season.

Fig 6—A general view of a cold frame used for seeds, showing evenness of frame if conditions are correct.

Fig 7—Plant potted up ready for planting out.

What is very difficult, is that each variety varies quite considerably in each garden according to its surroundings. By this I mean that you might select a dozen varieties of the same height, and in some seasons they might all vary, whereas a block of one variety would probably match up. With the early, mid-season and late varieties it is possible to have an all-blue border, which would give you a good display over a long period. This could be graded from the very dark varieties down to the very pale blue, and could equally apply to the pale mauves contrasting with the deep purples.

On the other hand, a good mixed bed can be very attractive, provided there are some good patches of the white varieties to split up the colours.

Lovely as such a border can be, one really associates delphiniums with a mixed herbaceous border, where they look so grand and stately among other perennials. Blue flowers are still very scarce, so that a family of plants producing so many different shades of blue, mauve and purple with variations of these shades, as well as white and pink, adds pleasure to the garden. This is especially so if the border has a fine background in the form of a green hedge or trees in the distance.

It is, of course, much easier if the entire border can be planted at the same time, whether one is using delphiniums alone or in a mixed bed. So often borders are begun with no plan at all, and in such cases it is rare for any of the plants to be seen at their best. The proper association of various plants is something which is now interesting gardeners more than ever before. Fortunately, there are so many really attractive herbaceous plants which fit in well with delphiniums. If these are carefully selected it will be possible not only to have some which will flower at the same time as delphiniums, but those which will be in colour earlier in the year as well as those which will grow up later and give a display in the autumn.

Every one of us will have our own ideas of what we wish to grow with our delphiniums, and it will not really be difficult to choose other plants that will add brightness to the garden when the delphiniums have finished flowering. Dahlias are valuable for this purpose, but to ensure success it is wise to grow them in 6-inch pots, so that they can be planted out when the delphiniums are over. It is little use planting your dahlias by the side of the delphiniums in the hope of their making a good show later, for the delphinium foliage would only suffocate them.

I would strongly recommend visiting one of the larger flower shows before making a choice of delphiniums, or, better still, visit one of the specialist's nurseries and choose your plants while they are in bloom. This also gives the opportunity of seeing their habit of growth, which is important for the purposes of a mixed border.

Quite a number of people are planting their borders with flowering shrubs, in order to cut down the labour in their gardens. Fortunately, there are a lot of shrubs which will live in happy association with delphiniums and other perennial plants. Particularly suitable for this purpose are the following, none of which has widespread roots, and they are therefore not likely to take the nourishment from the soil which is needed by delphiniums.

> *Amelanchier laevis*, white.
> *Berberis stenophylla*, yellow.
> *Ceanothus floribundus*, blue.
> *Cytisus praecox*, yellow.
> *Deutzia gracilis rosea*, pink.
> *Forsythia intermedia*, yellow.
> *Kerria japonica*, yellow.
> *Kolkwitzia amabilis*, pink.

Philadelphus coronarius, cream.
Prunus blireiana, pink, dark foliage.
Ribes sanguineum, light red.
Rose species, yellow, white, pink.

Since most of the flowering shrubs bloom in the spring, this means that there is very little colour later in the year. It is therefore a good idea to leave bays in a shrub border, where groups of delphiniums can be planted. These will give a great deal of pleasure, as otherwise this part of the garden, while giving a lovely display in the spring, could be very dull for the rest of the year.

Although delphiniums look so lovely wherever they are grown, care must, of course, be taken in the choice of varieties and colours, for both the mixed herbaceous and the shrub border.

Depending on the background, it is advisable to use the lighter shades towards the rear of the border, with the darker tones nearer the middle. The final choice will obviously depend on the local surroundings, while every one of us has his personal preferences.

Wherever they are used, delphiniums must be carefully looked after if they are to produce the best results. This includes thinning out the clumps to about four strong shoots, feeding and watering them, keeping the stems staked and, as necessary, taking steps to deal with mildew and slugs. If the central spikes are removed before they begin to form seed pods, the lateral growths will soon produce colour, and so lengthen the flowering period.

For general garden display the laterals on the main spikes need not be removed, as is done when growing for exhibition.

⟫ 5 ⟪

Growing for Exhibition

∞∞∞∞∞∞∞∞∞∞∞∞∞∞∞∞∞∞∞∞∞∞

NOT SO MANY YEARS AGO the delphinium was only rarely to be seen exhibited at horticultural shows. It has now become much more used at flower shows, and is proving to be a grand subject for this purpose.

While in the initial stages the culture of plants grown to produce exhibition flowers is the same as that given for garden display, there are a few extra attentions needed. It is essential to begin with really good plants from which only three or four young growths are allowed to mature. These shoots should be carefully selected and be spaced and tied out individually, as necessary.

The plants are fed and watered as mentioned previously, not forgetting to grow them in soil containing lime, for they do not like acid conditions. Hydrated lime is best for heavy ground, carbonate of lime on light soil. Use 3 to 4 ounces to the square yard, lightly pricking it into the surface soil.

In order to help really good spikes to develop, it will be found useful to give a feed of a general fertiliser about ten days after applying the dried blood recommended for general culture. I mention this because in some seasons we have a very cold period, which is sometimes wet and sometimes dry, during the early part of the growing season, and this can be very damaging. Growth is checked by the dryness, and the plants become hard and stunted as a result. If you can manage to keep the plants growing during these difficult times, you will find it has a great bearing on the results later on.

Keep the ground moving all the time in the early period, and keep removing any surplus growths. When the spikes begin to form, see that they are kept well watered. If the soil is of a light texture, a good mulch is of very great assistance in maintaining the moisture in the soil, and it also acts as a very good cover to the surface roots during a hot spell, which is quite likely at this time of the year.

It will be necessary, when the spikes are forming, to feed the plants with sulphate of potash. Use about a large teaspoonful to each plant, and apply it carefully right round the plant, and then water it in. This will tend to harden up the stems and steady the growth of the plant, which is sometimes inclined to rush ahead too fast. If it does this, then long, fleshy spikes will result that can be very badly twisted by the wind while they are in the process of forming. The flowers, too, become very badly spaced.

When the flowers are required for exhibition, it is important to ensure that all the goodness goes into the main spike on each shoot, since that is what you will be exhibiting. For this purpose the laterals which often form at the base of the spike should be removed. When the plants are grown for garden and house decoration the laterals can, of course, be left. In this case when the central spike has finished it can be removed, then the laterals will come into their own, and lengthen the flowering period, providing that extra bit of colour in the garden.

One point, however, which must not be overlooked at the present time, is that the Delphinium Society still considers that two small laterals should be left on each spike. Under this rule, if two entries were about equal in quality, the scales would weigh in favour of the exhibitor who had not removed all the laterals.

Obviously, it is important to select the very best spikes available for exhibition. It is essential that the bottom florets on the spike should be fresh, with the petals firmly held.

People will sometimes say that this does not matter, and that the lower florets can easily be removed if they look 'tired' or faded, and no one will know. However, this will easily be detected by the judges, and such treatment does, of course, tend to make the spike look rather leggy in appearance, as well as lowering its quality in the eyes of the judges.

Remember that you require as much of the spike to be in flower as possible, the colour must be good and, above all, the florets must be evenly placed. When you are cutting your flowers for the show, always cut them in the cool of the evening or first thing in the morning and place in deep containers.

As regards transport, if you can carry the flowers in water, so much the better. All my flowers travel in water, and that is a great help, but of course I quite realise that most amateurs cannot arrange that, so they have to improvise. The flowers should have the base of the stems blocked with cotton wool while under water, so that they hold the moisture. Wrap each spike in tissue paper and lay flat in a box or on the floor of your car, if the seats can be removed.

On arrival at the exhibition hall, the flowers should immediately be unpacked. Remove the tissue paper, turn the spike upside down, take out the cotton wool and fill up the stem with water. Then put a finger or thumb over the stem and submerge it in a deep container of water before removing the finger. The stem should then be full of water. Do this carefully with each spike, and after a good drink you should then start to stage your spikes in their right classes.

Where the schedule calls for three or five spikes, do try to match them up well, for an unbalanced exhibit does tend to spoil the effect, and valuable points are lost in consequence. See that the vase is well weighted. I do not like to see the stems cut too short, as it detracts from the exhibit if the bottom florets are only a few inches above the vase.

On the other hand, one has to be careful that the exhibit is not top heavy, as then it is liable to topple over. This can damage your entry and also cause harm to other competitors. It would be very unfortunate if this should happen just before judging, and after the hall had been cleared. It would then be very difficult for the judges to arrive at a fair decision.

When the class calls for only one spike, see that the bloom is well wedged in the vase with reeds or moss, etc. Label your exhibits carefully, for I do feel that entries that are not labelled tend to detract from the general interest of the show, especially as far as the gardening public is concerned. This is a great pity, for all societies must create as much public interest as possible, otherwise they will soon find that the shows will not get the support they deserve, with the result that they will be run at a loss. That, in turn, may mean the curtailing of one or more shows in a season, which would cause disappointment to many people.

❧ 6 ❧

Delphiniums for Home Decoration

‹∞∞∞∞∞∞∞∞∞∞∞∞∞∞∞∞∞∞∞∞∞∞∞∞∞∞∞∞∞∞›

D URING RECENT YEARS interest in floral arrangement has increased tremendously, and many flowers once rarely considered as being suitable for indoor decoration have proved to be ideal for that purpose. Delphiniums in particular have become almost an essential part in the make-up of summer arrangements, for they, like gladioli, give length and breadth. Much of the present enthusiasm is due to the most lovely displays which have been seen at the Delphinium Society's shows.

The lovely arrangements of cut delphiniums that can be staged are really breath-taking, both when used on their own and when arranged with other flowers.

While they are in season, delphiniums must be considered as almost indispensable to the flower arranger, especially in massed and large arrangements, where they supply the essential towering line. There has been such a big advancement of the flower during the last thirty years that we can now have spikes of 2 or 4 feet of actual flowers. Individual florets are now sometimes as much as 3 to $3\frac{1}{2}$ inches in diameter, with long pedicels or stalks, so that they can be taken off any spikes one does not wish to cut and used as a flower in themselves, which gives a new angle. There are of course very many florets on each spike, so that variety can be secured with little trouble, for there is no other flower in which so many shades of blue are to be found as well as other colours.

38

PLATE V A striking arrangement for a corner

Then of course the laterals can be used. These are often at their peak as the main spike is passing its best or after it has been cut. Used by themselves they are choice, but when included in mixed arrangements they give a gracefulness and lightness which would otherwise be missing.

With forethought in selecting varieties and with rotation of cropping it is possible to have delphiniums in colour from June (earlier if a glasshouse is available) to early November. First you have the main plants, then your first flowers from your seedlings, then your cuttings.

Until one seriously begins to consider the colour range in delphiniums, it is impossible to imagine the many shades available. Apart from the almost unbelievable number of blue and purple shades, there are many 'shot' or overlaid with pink, all with differently coloured eyes or 'bees' as they are known.

Then there are the pink shades which go from palest blush to a plum colour, and a number of good white-flowered varieties. The latter are excellent not only because when growing they brighten the garden, but used indoors they stand out well against dark backgrounds. They are made especially attractive by their dark-shaded centres.

Some of the palest lavender varieties give an almost grey effect, an invaluable colour in the hands of the skilled flower arranger.

The different shades in one flower of many of the varieties enables them to be used in so many ways and to pick up the colour of other flowers being used in an arrangement. There is, for instance, the rosy flush on some of the pale blues, plum shading on bright blue and in some cases a glistening shot effect. Then there are florets with pale centres, and a few with deeper-edged petals. Some are single, others semi-double or fully

C   41

PLATE VI A close-up section of 'Kent Messenger'
PLATE VII A close-up section of 'Twertonian'
PLATE VIII General view of delphiniums in full bloom

double. The shape of the petals also varies from being rounded to quite pointed, while a few varieties are nicely waved.

It is wise to remember that under artificial light some of the colour of the blues and mauves is 'lost', so that if delphiniums are being used for a dinner-table, the rosy-mauves, pinks, heliotropes and plum-flushed varieties should be chosen. These colours also fit in well with the table silver.

We must not overlook the fact that delphinium seed heads are very useful as a dried decoration and look especially good seen in an arrangement of mixed dried flowers and seed pods. It is also possible to dry the actual flowers and have colour in winter.

As a rule, of course, it is advisable to remove seed pods before they develop, but if just a few are saved, they will prove their worth during the winter.

The belladonna varieties, the small-flowered type, are especially suitable for floral arrangement work, whether one is seeking to make an interesting decoration for the living-room or intends competing in an exhibition class.

While they have not the height or massiveness of the elatum varieties, the belladonnas impart a gracefulness, which otherwise is so often lacking.

Not all flowers are really suitable for arranging in a bowl on a pedestal. The delphinium is ideal for this purpose. The spikes can be the secondary ones or laterals from the main spikes, while individual florets can also be used.

One of the most delightful examples I have seen of such an arrangement contained stems of flowers from the lime tree, which had been denuded of their leaves, with spikes of the lovely gentian blue delphinium 'Anne Page'. These were all secondary spikes, very graceful, and flowering right down over the front of the bowl, and thereby creating a very pleasing effect.

Another excellent combination was a big brass container which was filled with pale Cambridge-blue delphiniums, madonna lilies and grey foliage. Yet another arrangement which stands out in my mind was a delightful basket containing three or four small purple spikes with primrose-coloured anthemis flowers, with leaves of *Acer negundo* used as a foil. I have also seen some other exquisite arrangements using very small laterals with other small flowers.

Delphiniums can also be arranged most successfully with favourite flowers such as gladioli, lilies, paeonies and sweet peas.

Whether used for informal or formal events, the delphinium is supreme during its flowering period, and the Society has shown on many occasions that while the flower has been cultivated and loved for centuries, it is a subject which can take and hold its place among the very best of our modern flowers.

At their 1958 show the Delphinium Society arranged two rooms, suitably furnished, the one for a wedding reception and the other as a living-room. This was at Mr and Mrs Parretts' home in Cobham, where the Surrey ladies put on a lovely floral display at the same time as the garden was open for the National Gardens' scheme. The whole effect was a grand success, and showed everyone who visited the house and garden how versatile a flower the modern delphinium is.

Then in 1959, when the Delphinium Society visited my nurseries near Maidstone, some of the members of the Society prepared some delightful arrangements in my own home, which is attached to the nurseries. As it was a very hot day, the beautiful blue arrangements were quite lovely, and gave great satisfaction to all.

It is important to cut the flowers at the right time, so that they remain colourful for a long period. If the spike is cut when the three or four lowest florets are open, it should ensure a prolonged display. When cutting for exhibition, the spike should have many florets open; in fact, with the best modern sorts the florets do open in fairly quick succession. Ideally for show work, the lower florets should still be in good condition when the topmost ones unfold.

Fortunately, the majority of the modern varieties do not quickly show signs of weather damage, which is something the raisers have always borne in mind when creating new sorts.

It is important to prevent delphiniums from flagging after they are cut. As soon as the spikes are severed, they should be plunged into water, for it is important to prevent an air-lock. If these form in the stem, water is prevented from reaching the florets and leaves, leading of course to wilting. If an interval is unavoidable between cutting and plunging into water, the base of the stem should be cut again and the spike immediately stood in deep water. Whenever possible, the cut should be made while the stem is actually held under water. This ensures that air-locks do not occur. Delphinium stems are more or less hollow, and are more likely to be so when growth has been quick and soft. It is a good plan to turn such spikes upside down and fill them with water. Then plug the base with cotton wool, a leaf or Florapak before placing it in water.

Should flagging occur at any time, the flowers can usually be revived by standing the base of the stem in boiling water. Keep them in a cool place in dull light for an hour or two, and usually they will recover and last a good time.

When finally arranging the spikes, some of which will have to be shortened, always make a slanting cut at the base. This exposes a large area of stem base to the water.

Careful handling at all times is necessary, since the florets bruise easily and it is not difficult to break the spikes, which should preferably always be stood upright while awaiting use.

This prevents bruising which may occur when stems are 'heaped' up.

Most people tend to think that delphiniums can only be used in large containers, which of course is true if you are going to confine yourself to exhibition spikes. However, the true exhibition flower does not actually make the best arrangement.

The delphinium today can be arranged in any type of container or vase, but the selection of the right one according to the sort of arrangement required can do much to enhance the value of the decoration. Bronze-coloured receptacles are particularly useful, while wide mouthed vases and large metal lined ornamental baskets can be used to make magnificent displays.

Stem holders are usually necessary, and they are available in many sizes. Some crumpled wire netting is a further aid, for it does help to set the stems at almost any angle.

Whether a small table, or even a wall vase, is to be filled, delphiniums can be used with great success, while a large container of stately spikes standing on the floor can be an imposing sight.

⤞ 7 ⤝

Delphiniums in August and September

‹‹‹‹‹‹‹‹‹‹‹‹‹‹‹‹‹‹‹‹‹‹‹‹‹‹‹‹‹‹‹

I HAVE BEEN EXPERIMENTING with the possibility of obtaining two crops of flowers in one season, and one summer I decided to put my experiment to the test.

I felt that if I succeeded it would give a great deal of pleasure to all delphinium lovers, for it would considerably extend the flowering period of this delightful plant.

My delphiniums flowered as usual, and they were kept constantly watered by the use of a spray line. I noticed that while the first flowers were in bloom the bases of most of the plants were making up very well. So I decided that part of the delphiniums were to be allowed to seed, but the remainder, consisting of about 4,000 plants, were to be cut right down as soon as they began to show their seed pods. Each variety was operated on in this way and all the plants received a good dressing of a well-balanced fertiliser. The plants were kept well watered and the surface soil was well worked to keep it perfectly clear of weeds. For nearly six weeks I had a glorious show of colour which would have carried on longer had I had enough water to have kept them growing. They were dusted twice with green sulphur to stop any possible attack of mildew, which is sometimes prevalent at this time of the year.

The plants were not thinned at all, only the laterals were

removed, many plants carrying as many as eight to ten spikes. The spikes were not quite so large as the first ones, but they were excellent for floral decoration work. I asked a prominent member of the Delphinium Society to come over and see my effort. He was quite amazed, as he came with the idea of possibly seeing a few odd spikes here and there.

The plants were allowed to ripen off gradually, taking care only to remove the flower spikes immediately after flowering, to stop seeding, thus allowing all possible sap to return to the crown, in order to build up the plant for another year. Some people rather feared that my plants might suffer and that the results obtained the next year would not be so good. However, when I had occasion to lift one or two plants, the crowns were full of strong eyes, which certainly augured well for the future.

The following year the plants bloomed magnificently and gained many good awards at the various shows, proving that the experiment had no adverse effects the year after.

A few important points emerge from this, as follows:
1. All flower spikes must be removed immediately they start to form seed pods.
2. Cut down immediately within 3 or 4 inches from the base.
3. Keep the plants well watered the whole time and do not allow them to become dry.
4. Give a good dressing of a well-balanced fertiliser.
5. Keep free from weeds and keep the top soil moving to let in the air.
6. Keep them tied up and remove all laterals.
7. Again remove the flowers as soon as any sign of seed pods develop.

8. Leave as much top growth as possible and only cut down when plants have practically died back, in order to let as much sap return to the crown.

Unless you are able to look after your delphiniums by feeding and watering after their first flowering, I would not recommend this drastic method. If you carried out these instructions on delphiniums which were planted in a main herbaceous border and were unable to keep them very well watered, the plants would probably dry up altogether, for you would be exposing the crown to the full heat of the sun, which might very well lead to complete loss.

⨠ 8 ⨟

Vegetative Propagation

∽∽∽∽∽∽∽∽∽∽∽∽∽∽∽∽∽∽∽∽∽∽

ALTHOUGH IT IS POSSIBLE to raise really good plants from seed, in order to increase the number of plants of a particular variety it is necessary either to take cuttings of young growths or divide the plants. By these means one can be sure of reproducing characteristics which certain plants exhibit. By far the best method is to take cuttings from the stock plants, for the results are much healthier than those obtained from plants that have been divided.

Many different types of cuttings are used in propagating plants, but for the majority of hardy perennials, including delphiniums, young soft growths are taken in the spring. There are two methods of doing this. The first is to lift the entire plant in the spring when the shoots have grown 3 or 4 inches high. Each of the shoots can be removed, taking care to see that each cutting is taken off with a firm base. It is best to avoid any cuttings of which the stems are hollow, for they do not generally root well. A clean cut should be made and the majority of the leaves carefully trimmed off. The more foliage that is left on, the longer the cuttings take to root. Once the base of the cutting has calloused over, no further nutriment can be taken up until fresh roots begin to form. The cuttings can become very withered at this stage, as will be seen in the photograph. So it is clearly important to remove as much foliage as possible.

It is always advisable to make a clean cut immediately below a joint, for it is at this point that roots form most readily. The base of all cuttings should be made perfectly smooth and clean. If left ragged, torn or bruised, rooting will be hindered or prevented altogether. This is because the strength of the cells will be diverted to healing injuries before beginning the process of making new roots.

This is why it is essential to use a really sharp knife when making the cuttings.

Having taken the main cuttings, the plant can be replanted and, if required, lifted again when another batch of suitable growths for cuttings have developed. You may, however, prefer to leave the plant as it is after the first lot of cuttings.

If a further batch of cuttings is taken, it is usual and wise to scrap the plant, which will by then have become quite weak.

A second method of securing cuttings is to leave the plant in the ground, and scrape away as much soil as possible from around it, so that the cuttings can be taken with a solid base.

Apart from the securing of cuttings, this method is a means of thinning out your shoots and making good use of them, instead of merely topping them and throwing them away.

The soil should be replaced immediately the cuttings have been removed, making sure that it is well firmed around the roots. Three or four good shoots should be left on each plant, and if looked after well, they will produce some really first-class spikes.

For rooting the cuttings, the mixture I prefer is equal parts of good soil, peat and silver sand. It is sometimes recommended to use only peat and sand, but neither of these contains any food value, although, of course, they are important, in fact almost essential, for the rooting of cuttings of all subjects. I include soil (or loam), since its use does enable the cuttings to grow, once roots form. The prepared cuttings can either be inserted into deep seed trays or into 3½-inch pots.

After being watered well, they should be placed immediately in a cold frame, of which the glass should be lightly shaded.

As far as possible, the cuttings should not be watered again until they have rooted, for they are best left on the dry side. Too much water in the early stages can cause quite a lot of damping off. On sunny days it may be necessary to increase the glass shading, and I have always found that the preparation known as Summer Cloud is excellent for painting on to the glass.

Once it becomes apparent that the cuttings are rooting—and this will be seen by their perky appearance—more ventilation must be given and the glass gradually removed. If it is left on too long, the young plants will become weak and leggy. When growth begins to develop, the rooted cuttings should be moved to 3½-inch pots using the John Innes Compost No. 1. Stand the plants in a closed cold frame for a few days until they have settled in the pots. Then gradually give them increased ventilation, at first only during daytime, until finally the glass can be removed altogether.

When the young plants are growing well, pinch out the growing points in order to encourage some good useful growth from the base of your plants. Move the plants when ready to the open ground into well-prepared soil. If you have no space available in which to set the plants when they are growing well, then move them to bigger pots, for the great point to remember is that on no account must they become pot bound or starved. Use the 5- or 6-inch pots and the John Innes Compost No. 2. This will keep the plants growing well and encourage the production of a really good crown for flowering the next year. This latter method is certainly one to be recommended, for if the plants are placed in these bigger pots, they

16511A

should be well established by the time you wish to plant out, in August or early September, when they can be moved without root disturbance.

Any flower buds which develop while the plants are in pots should be removed, in order that the strength of the plant can be devoted to building up good flowering growths for the next season.

The best time to propagate delphiniums by division is in the spring, in fact it is the only satisfactory time. If the operation is attempted in the autumn, it is practically certain that all of the divisions will perish. Growth ceases to be active during winter months, and therefore it is quite reasonable to anticipate that autumn-made divisions are unlikely to root, but will most probably rot away, especially on a wet, heavy clay soil.

From the middle of February onwards is the time to divide delphiniums, the exact time depending, of course, on weather conditions and whether the varieties to be propagated are early, mid-season or late flowering.

Lift the plants carefully and wash all the soil off. Then take a sharp knife and cut the plants up into separate pieces, each with one or two good crowns. Having done this, dip the divisions into a box of powdered charcoal, so that all the cut areas are really covered with the powder. Then lay the divisions in a box in the cool greenhouse or a shed for a day or two, to allow the cut surfaces to dry. When these are dry, the divisions are planted in the normal way.

With this treatment there will be little likelihood of black rot developing. This is a most troublesome disease, which, if it gains a hold, can soon work through an entire stock of plants and prove quite disastrous.

As a general rule, plants raised from cuttings are seldom attacked by black rot and this is one important reason why the division of delphiniums cannot be recommended without reserve. It is certainly unwise to divide plants too frequently, for when this is done there is always the possibility of the entire stock breaking down.

The weakening of the plants will occur if the divisions should 'bleed', and delphiniums do tend to bleed badly when cut up. This is the main reason why it is essential to see that the cut surfaces have dried up before they are planted. Naturally, a weak plant is more susceptible to black rot and similar trouble.

There is another important point to remember when planting delphiniums, whether one is planting up divisions, young plants or older specimens, and that is that they must be firmly embedded in the soil. So many people, whether they are planting out or potting up young plants, do tend to carry out this operation far too loosely. Loose planting leads to the drying of the roots and also prevents the roots from gaining a hold. This is why a trowel or spade should be used for planting, while the soil should be worked between and over the roots, so that there is close contact between the two and no possibility of the roots being suspended in 'mid air'.

I am sure loose planting is a very frequent cause of losses.

⪼ 9 ⪻

Propagation from Seed

⟨∼∼∼∼∼∼∼∼∼∼∼∼∼∼∼∼∼∼∼∼∼∼∼∼∼⟩

FOR THOSE WHO DO NOT WISH to buy the named varieties, a great deal of pleasure can be derived from growing delphiniums from seed. Some gardeners like to sow their seed in August, soon after it has ripened on the plants for delphinium seed does not germinate freely if it is kept too long. However, if the seed is kept in a refrigerator until it is required for sowing, it will germinate as freely as if sown in the late summer. This is very helpful, because when the seed is sown in the summer the resultant plants are not very big by the time the dormant season arrives and they are not so easily wintered. I prefer to sow my seed in a cold house or frame about the end of February or early March. One has then a longer season for growing, with the result that some first-class plants can be obtained. These can be planted out in their flowering quarters so that a selection can be made the following year.

It is from this method of careful selection that it is always possible that one may be able to select a new variety. If the variety is considered good enough, cuttings can be taken the following year, as in the case of the named varieties. Then, if it is still outstanding, three spikes can be put before the Joint Delphinium Committee at the Royal Horticultural Society's Hall, Vincent Square, London, and if judged good enough, the variety may be given an Award of Merit for exhibition or be selected for trial at the Society's gardens, Wisley, Surrey, where a Trial of Delphiniums is held annually. Here it will be judged as a garden plant, and may obtain an award of merit or be highly commended. All the varieties receiving an award of merit in London when shown as a cut flower are automatically sent to Wisley for trial.

Having dealt with the possible results that can be obtained by raising delphiniums from seed, I will now try to give you a few details as to how to grow them.

The seeds should be sown in seed trays, which should contain the John Innes Seed Compost, and the whole contents should be well firmed. Sow very thinly and cover the seeds very lightly. When the seeds are sown too deep, you will find that very few, if any, will germinate. Give the boxes a good watering and do not water again unless absolutely necessary, or the seedlings may damp off.

Cover the boxes with brown paper or a piece of sacking, as the seed will germinate better in the dark. Once the seeds start to germinate, the paper covering can be removed. As soon as the seedlings are big enough to handle, lift them very carefully, in order not to disturb the late starters, and either put them into little pots or prick them out into a prepared bed. Later on, if you can spare the room, I would suggest that the seedlings should be planted out in rows at a distance of 6 to 9 inches apart. Now I know that some gardeners will say that this distance is rather close, but don't forget that you will be very lucky if you are able to pick out many winners that are likely to equal the name sorts. Some of these plants will probably throw a flower spike in the late summer, and if they are allowed to bloom you will probably be able to weed out the poorest plants, which will automatically give more room to the remainder for another season.

Strictly speaking, these first blooms should be cut off in the early stages, so that a good crown can be built up for flowering the next season. If part of the spike is allowed to flower, however, one can form some idea of what the plant is worth, and, as I have said previously, the poor ones can be removed. If space is not of paramount importance, do not remove any plants unless you have to, for one cannot always be certain of what results will follow from the small spikes the first season. All that is then required is to keep the hoe going in order to free the plants from weeds and the soil from drying out, keeping them well watered as necessary.

From the time the seedlings are first planted, be sure to dust the ground regularly with slug powder, or slugs may devour your best plants. By the next spring, it will be noticed that the foliage of all the plants will vary in colour, and that will give you an idea as to the colour of the flowers. The dark blue or purple delphiniums have dark foliage or red stems, while the pale blue, mauve, mid-blue or white ones have light-coloured stems and leaves.

Variety will not end there, because in your collection you will probably have early, mid-season and late varieties, which all help to lengthen the period of flowering.

If you grow delphiniums from seed, do purchase your stock from a specialist firm, or from an amateur who has a first-class named collection, as otherwise you will not get such a good selection of colours or forms.

When the plants are in full flower is the time to select the specimens to keep and propagate for another season. Quite rightly, anyone growing delphiniums for the first time will immediately ask, 'What have I to look for in a good delphinium?'

Undoubtedly colour must play a very important part and, of course, everyone has a different approach to this subject. As

FIG 8—Delphiniums grown from seed, showing evenness of germination.

FIG 9—General view of field planted in early May before staking.

FIG 10—'Valentia'—lobelia blue shaded amethyst.

FIG 11—'Bridesmaid'—silvery mauve with white eye.

far as I am concerned I feel that the individual floret is very much linked up with colour. Most of the modern delphiniums have really large florets, 3 inches or more in diameter, with bees or eyes in various shades of brown, black and white, which help to set off the flower. These florets are not just a single row of petals 1 inch in diameter, which are sometimes hooded. They have two or three rows of petals, thereby making a bold flower in themselves. The plant should produce a strong spike, which is sometimes in the form of a pyramid, the base of the spike being much broader than the top, or it can be just a straight spike. Apart from the spike, the next most important point is the placing of the florets on the stem. They should face outwards and be evenly spaced on the stem, and not gappy.

Once satisfied that the colour, florets and the spike are right, we have to consider the lasting qualities. A good modern delphinium should not drop its bottom florets before the top ones are open, for that is a bad point. There are perfect delphiniums which produce small florets only and they also have a place in the garden as a cut flower.

Delphiniums vary considerably in height according to their surroundings, which may be very sheltered and warm, so don't get too alarmed at the height of your seedlings, as this may be due to being too close in the seedling bed. Young plants will be shorter when they are grown from cuttings and are given more room.

I hope that I have given some idea of what we should all try to look for in a delphinium.

However, if you are ever in doubt, never hesitate to contact a keen grower in your district who will be able to put you on the right track. Remember that the most important points are:

1. Sow the seed very thinly.
2. Cover the seed very lightly.
3. Keep the light away from the seed until it germinates.
4. Keep the compost watered, never allow it to dry out.
5. Never allow high temperatures in the greenhouse.

❧ 10 ❦

Some Recommended Varieties

⌒⌒⌒⌒⌒⌒⌒⌒⌒⌒⌒⌒⌒⌒⌒⌒⌒⌒⌒⌒⌒

THERE IS NOW A VERY LARGE NUMBER of really first-class varieties readily available, and I believe that those I now mention include all the very finest sorts. They are all varieties I have grown, so that I have personally been able to assess their qualities. Some are older than others, and though the cost of the plants as offered by the specialist growers does vary considerably, there are plants priced to suit all pockets.

One of the reasons why delphiniums sometimes seem dearer than some other perennial plants, is that they do not increase so quickly. This, eventually at least, is an advantage, for it does mean that they do not spread rapidly and occupy more than their allotted space, as do some herbaceous subjects.

There is, of course, considerable variation in all shades of blue, but the following table of varieties gives the main shades.

The letters E, M and L indicate that a variety is early, mid-season or late flowering.

LARGE FLOWERED ELATUM SECTION

PALE MAUVE

Bee Elliott (M)	Silvery mauve with white eye. 6 ft.
Melora (M)	Very pale mauve with white eye. 5 ft.
Bridesmaid (M)	Silvery mauve with white eye. 6 ft.
Constance Marment (M)	Silvery mauve with white eye, similar to Bridesmaid but florets are shaped differently. 6 ft.
Lady Guinevere (E)	Pale mauve with white eye. 5 ft.
Nell Gwynn (L)	Rosy mauve. $5\frac{1}{2}$ ft.
Margaret Farrand (M)	Light mauve with white eye. $5\frac{1}{2}$ ft.
Olivia (M)	Lilac mauve with white eye. $5\frac{1}{2}$ ft.

DEEP MAUVE

Porthos (M)	Lavender mauve with dark eye. 6 ft.
Twertonian (M)	Deep mauve with blue shadings and white eye. $5\frac{1}{2}$ ft.
Julia Langdon (M)	Mauve with blue sheen and white eye. 5 ft.
Great Britain (M)	Light cobalt-violet with white eye. 5 ft.
Cinderella (M)	Light heliotrope with brown eye. $3\frac{1}{2}$ to 4 ft.
Judy Knight (M)	True heliotrope with black eye. 5 ft.

VIOLET TO PURPLE

Father Thames (M)	Rosy violet and gentian-blue. 5 ft.
Cynthia Bishop (M)	Velvety violet with dark eye. $4\frac{1}{2}$ ft.

Purple Prince (M)	Purple self. This may also produce purple flowers with white eye, especially in the autumn. 5 ft.
Purple Triumph (M)	Rich violet purple with black and gold eye. 5 ft.
Guy Langdon (M)	Rich royal-purple with purple and white eye. 5 ft.
Minerva (M)	Deep violet with black and gold eye. 5 ft.
Evelyn Ogg (M)	Rich purple-mauve with white eye. 6 ft.
Beau Nash (M)	Purple and dark mauve with black and gold eye. $5\frac{1}{2}$ ft.
Kent Messenger (M)	Deep bluish purple with gentian-blue markings with bold white eye. 6 ft.
Royal Marine (M)	Fine deep purple with white eye. 5 ft.

ROSY VIOLET TO PURPLE

Wessex (M)	Rosy purple with brown eye. 5 ft.
Mogul (M)	Rosy purple with white eye. 6 ft.
Minstrel Boy (M)	Rich amethyst-violet with black, brown and gold eye. $3\frac{1}{2}$ to 4 ft.

DARK BLUE

Duchess of Portland (M)	Ultramarine-blue with white eye. 5 ft.
Eva Gower (M)	Deep blue with rose shadings. 5 ft.
Royalist (M)	Fine deep blue with white eye. 6 ft.

Supreme (M) — Aconite-violet and gentian-blue with bold white eye. 5 ft.

Jack Tar (L) — Very deep cornflower-blue deepening towards edges of florets with dark eye. 5 ft.

Côte d'Azure (M) — Dark gentian-blue with white eye. $5\frac{1}{2}$ ft.

GENTIAN-BLUE

Bleu Celeste (L) — Light gentian-blue with white eye. 6 ft.

Anne Page (M) — Deep gentian-blue with dark eye. 5 ft.

Neptune (L) — Marine-blue shaded mauve with white eye. 6 ft.

Lady Wightman (M) — Deep blue with white eye. 6 ft.

Lorna (M) — Deep blue with dark brown eye. 5 ft.

Valentia (M) — Lobelia-blue shaded with amethyst. $6\frac{1}{2}$ ft.

Gladys Sharp (M) — Bright gentian-blue, flushed with rosy mauve. 5 ft.

Mermaid (L) — Deep blue with white eye. $4\frac{1}{2}$ ft.

Ivy Ridgewell (M) — Deep cornflower-blue with white eye. 6 ft.

Star of Eve (M) — Deep cobalt-blue with white eye. 5 ft.

Charon (M) — Pure gentian-blue with black eye. $4\frac{1}{2}$ ft.

MID-BLUE

Marion (M) — Deep sky-blue with white eye. 5 ft.

Blackmore's Blue (M)	Lovely sky-blue with white eye. 5 ft.
Conquest (L)	Deep cornflower-blue with white eye. 5 ft.
Sonata (M)	Pale sky-blue with white eye. 5 ft.
Derek Hotblack (E)	Deep sky-blue with slight white eye. 5 ft.
Destiny (M)	French-blue with white eye. $5\frac{1}{2}$ ft.
Moon Rocket (L)	Mid-blue with white eye. 5 ft.
Daily Express (M)	Bright sky-blue with black and gold eye. 5 ft.
Isla (M)	Dove-blue with golden-brown eye. 5 ft.
Maid of Bath (M)	Oriental blue with white eye. 5 ft.
Agnes Brooks (M)	Gentian-blue with blue and white eye. 6 ft.
Dame Myra Curtis (L)	Sky-blue with blue and black eye. 5 ft.

PALE BLUE

Crystal (E)	Pale sky-blue with white eye. 6 ft.
Flora Campbell (L)	Attractive sky-blue with white eye. $5\frac{1}{2}$ ft.
Anona (M)	Very pale blue with slight mauve shadings and small white eye. 5 ft.
Sea Mist (M)	Clear pale blue with fine white eye. $5\frac{1}{2}$ ft.
Ena (M)	Pale Cambridge-blue with light brown eye. $4\frac{1}{2}$ ft.
Horizon (L)	Pale blue with tinges of mauve with white eye. 6 ft.

Oenone Lang (M)	Sky-blue with white eye. 5 ft.
Charles F. Langdon (E)	Pure blue with striking black eye. 6 ft.
Blue Beauty (M)	Pure blue with black eye. 5 ft.

PALE BLUE AND MAUVE

Audrey Mott (L)	Sky-blue with mauve and deep blue shadings. 5 ft.
Mazurka (M)	Blue with slight mauve shadings with blue and black eye. $5\frac{1}{2}$ ft.
Wild Wales (M)	Forget-me-not blue with heavy mauve shadings with black eye. 5 ft.
Alice Artingdale (M)	Light-blue and mauve shadings. 5 ft.
Lady Eleanor (M)	Light sky-blue shaded mauve. 6 ft.
Nora O'Fallon (M)	Clear pale blue with striking black eye. $5\frac{1}{2}$ ft.

PALE MAUVE AND BLUE

Mrs Newton Lees (E)	Pale mauve and blue, with slight black eye. 5 ft.
Lady Dorothy (M)	Pale mauve and blue with black eye. $5\frac{1}{2}$ ft.
Oberon (L)	Mauve and blue with deeper centre. $5\frac{1}{2}$ ft.
Jennifer Langdon (E)	Pale mauve and blue with striking black eye. 5 ft.
Titania (L)	Rose-lavender and sky-blue with black eye. 5 ft.
Bowdon Girl (M)	Lavender-mauve and blue with very striking black eye. 5 ft.

PLATE IX A close-up of 'Mazurka'
PLATE X A close-up of 'Daily Express'

SOME RECOMMENDED VARIETIES

MAUVE AND PALE BLUE

Silver Moon (M)	Silvery mauve and slight blue shading with white eye. 5 ft.
Laura Fairbrother (L)	True mauve with sky-blue shading and tiny white eye. 7 ft.
Gertrude Raphael (L)	Pale mauve and blue with black eye. 6 ft.

DEEP MAUVE AND BLUE

W. B. Cranfield (M)	Gentian-blue and mauve with white eye. 5 ft.

DEEP PURPLE AND BLUE

Peacock (M)	Deep blue and purple with dark eye. $5\frac{1}{2}$ ft.
Dora Cairncross (M)	Cornflower-blue and violet-purple with sepia eye. $5\frac{1}{2}$ ft.
Fred Yule (M)	Deep blue and purple with black eye. $5\frac{1}{2}$ ft.
Purple Ruffles (L)	Deep purple and royal blue. $5\frac{1}{2}$ ft.

PINK

Tilly Knight (M)	Fine dusky pink with light brown eye. $5\frac{1}{2}$ ft.

WHITE

Janice (M)	Pure white. $3\frac{1}{2}$ to 4 ft.
Swan Lake (E)	Greyish-white with striking black eye. $5\frac{1}{2}$ ft.
Everest (M)	Fine white with white eye. 5 ft.
Charles Neaves (M)	Pure white. $4\frac{1}{2}$ ft.

PLATE XI A close-up of 'Julia Langdon'
PLATE XII A close-up of 'Dora Cairncross'

It may seem from the descriptions that there are many varieties in each section that must be identical in colour. To a great extent this is true, but it must be remembered that we have three distinct periods of flowering—early (mid-June), mid-season (late June) and late (early July)—which prolongs the show of colour of this popular flower.

In some seasons there is not a great distinction between the early and mid-season varieties, especially if any of the sections should hit a heat-wave. There is, of course, a difference in the formation of the spikes as well as the form of the individual florets.

BELLADONNA SECTION

Belladonna delphiniums are the small-flowered type which produce spikes of from 12 to 18 inches in length. They are very free flowering, and commence to bloom early in June. If carefully fed and looked after, they should flower most of the summer.

Most of the named varieties are very sparse as regards seeding, which is somewhat different from the Elatum strain. This may account for the relatively few named varieties in cultivation.

PALE BLUE

Blue Bees	Pale blue with white eye. $3\frac{1}{2}$ ft.
Capri	Pale Cambridge-blue with white eye. $3\frac{1}{2}$ ft.
Fernleigh Beauty	Pale blue with white eye. $3\frac{1}{2}$ ft.

PALE BLUE AND MAUVE

Semi-Plena	Sky-blue with mauve shadings. $3\frac{1}{2}$ ft.

MID-BLUE

Orion	Clear blue with white eye. 4 ft.
Theodora	Bright blue. 3 ft.

DARK BLUE AND MAUVE

Wendy	Gentian-blue and purple. $4\frac{1}{2}$ ft.

DARK BLUE

    Azure Queen   Dark blue. $3\frac{1}{2}$ ft.
    Bonita   Pure gentian-blue. 4 ft.
    Lamartine   Darkest blue in this section with
                            white eye. $3\frac{1}{2}$ ft.

WHITE

    Moerheimii   Pure white. $3\frac{1}{2}$ ft.

PINK

    Pink Sensation   Light rose-pink. $2\frac{1}{2}$ to 3 ft.

Hybridising Delphiniums

~~~~~~

MOST NEW VARIETIES of delphiniums are the results of cross fertilisation or hybridisation, which in reality means the crossing of one hybrid delphinium with another. The chief object of this work is to improve the standard of existing varieties.

I think it is true to say that, by and large, most of the hybridising has been carried out by members of the trade, such as Blackmore and Langdon, Reinelt, Samuelson and the late Frank Bishop of Bakers.

These firms produce their own strains, which are quite distinct, and vary considerably according to the different parts of the world in which they are raised in order to suit local requirements.

By this I mean that Blackmore and Langdon, and also the late Frank Bishop, aimed at raising perennial varieties, which have been known to remain in one position for many years without being moved. I think that the record at present must be held by a plant of the popular 'Lady Eleanor', which remained in the same position for close on thirty years. On the other hand, Reinelt of the U.S.A. developed a strain which is treated more as an annual or biennial, for it was very difficult to winter delphiniums successfully in his part of the world.

Considerable concern was felt over here after World War II that if the 'Pacific' strain of delphiniums was pursued too strongly, the delphinium might lose its perenniality. However, largely due to the fine work put in by the Delphinium Society, amateur members are now turning their attention to raising new really perennial varieties, in addition to the famous commercial firms in this country. It is hardly necessary to say that before commencing to cross two varieties, one should have some definite object in mind. This may be to obtain a new colour tone, larger spikes or florets, or perhaps to introduce scent or some other characteristic.

Most of us have our own idea as to what is the perfect delphinium, and we shall, therefore, all be looking to achieve the same object, but by different means. It is very probable that many crosses will be made before there are any worthwhile results, but if and when we do secure a 'break', the reward more than outweighs previous disappointments.

To go through the process briefly, we start by selecting two parents, chosen because of some distinctive quality. The male organ consists of the stamens which carry the pollen in little sacs known as anthers. When ripe, the anthers burst and release the pollen. The female organ consists of the pistil, at the end of which is the stigma, on to which the pollen grains must fall so that they can work their way into the miniature seed pod and fertilise the undeveloped seed. Since there are both pistil and stigmata on the same flower, it will be necessary to remove the latter to prevent self-fertilisation. When cross-fertilising, the female or seed parent must be young, for if it has reached full development it may either be self-fertilised or cross-fertilised by insects or wind.

Choose a basal floret which is just starting to open, and with the thumb and fingers fold back and hold the sepals in one hand and remove the 'eye' petals with a pair of tweezers or small pen-knife with the other hand.

Once these petals have been removed, the unripe anthers will be easily discernible. These should also be carefully removed in order not to damage the pistil. This operation having been carried out, the floret which is to be the seed parent should have been successfully emasculated.

Then select a floret from the variety from which you wish to make your cross; this should be taken off from approximately two-thirds of the way up the spike, if the pollen is right.

It is only necessary to remove the eye petals (corolla) so that the anthers can be seen. Fold back the sepals and carefully bring the anthers into contact with the stigma of the seed parent.

Pollination should be completed, so as soon as possible after the florets have been emasculated, and to make sure that the stigma has been receptive and taken the pollen, a small magnifying glass is a very useful aid, as it is not always possible to see this with the naked eye.

There are several theories as to when is the right time of the day to tackle this job, but as a general rule I would say that round about mid-day is probably the best time, but on no account carry out any crossing when the weather is showery.

Now that we have varieties flowering over a long period, I would recommend to a beginner that a start be made early in the season. Then, if the first crosses are unsuccessful, it will be possible to carry out further experiments.

If the cross has been successful, the seed pod will soon begin to swell, usually within a week or ten days.

The reason for choosing the basal florets for your seed parent is that the seed which is obtained from these lower flowers is always so much more mature.

It is generally considered advisable to make your cross each way, as the cross may be more successful one way than the other. That is, use flowers from the same two varieties as both male and female parents.

I also think that, to be on the safe side, each cross should be protected by muslin to keep out any insects.

If any of my readers wish to go more fully into plant breeding I would recommend W. J. C. Lawrence's book on *Practical Plant Breeding*, which deals fully with the subject.

When making a selection of the seedlings, as a result of your crossing, it is essential that you harden your heart and become ruthless, for there is always the tendency to think that all of one's seedlings are perfect.

It you are a little uncertain as to what to keep, enlist another enthusiast's opinion, for two heads are always better than one.

Having selected your best seedlings, it is necessary to grow them on and to take some cuttings the next spring. After trying them out for a couple of years or so, you will then have to make an even more drastic selection. Only the best is good enough to retain. It is no use going on with a new variety unless it is better than those already on the market.

The most important points to work for are:

A *Improvement* on existing varieties.
B Distinct break in colour or an improvement in colour.
C Good habit.
D True perennial character.
E Resistance to mildew.

Most raisers keep a book, where they write down particulars of all the crosses they have made and later record the results from each.

This is very important because some varieties are much better parents than others, and it is a great help to have this for future work.

FIG 12—An arrangement for the centre of a dining room table using mainly laterals.

FIG 13—An arrangement in a tea-caddy using the variety 'Silver Moon', mauve sweet peas and Begonia Rex.

FIG 14—A delightful small arrangement of pale blue delphinium 'Sonata', pink roses and white Jasmine.

FIG 15—A very light arrangement using only florets of varieties 'Mazurka' and 'Laura Fairbrother' with *Prunus pissardii* as foliage.

≫ 12 ≪

Diseases and Pests

IT IS NOW RECOGNISED that the delphinium is liable to be attacked by virus diseases in the same way as dahlias, chrysanthemums and other well-known flowers. However, virus is not so prevalent in this country, due to the fact that the aphis family does not care very much for the delphinium. This, of course, is a very different case from that of the dahlia. The aphides that attack the dahlia carry the infection to clean plants, so that as a preventative measure a nicotine spray in liquid or dust form should be used to keep this pest down. The virus that attacks the delphinium is the cucumber mosaic variety and is probably caused by thrip. It is quite easily discernible, as the affected growth is quite different from that of the parent plant. The leaves are generally more pointed, very irregular in shape and are also very blotchy. Growth is also weak and the flower is poor both in texture and colour, while the florets have a very shrivelled appearance.

An affected plant is not always completely overcome by this disease. It generally occurs on one, or perhaps two, shoots on a clump. These parts should be cut off and burnt as soon as noticed, and the plant marked either for destruction or at any rate as not to be used for future propagation, since this disease is so easily spread. If any of these plants should produce virus shoots the following year, they should certainly be destroyed, in

E   81

order to remove any further possibility of the disease being spread to healthy plants.

Black root rot is another disease that has given quite a lot of trouble both to trade growers as well as to amateurs. I think it is fair to say that this fungus attacks the roots of the plants during the winter months, but the authorities are not at the moment able to pin it down to one particular cause.

My own opinion, for what it is worth, is that the condition of the soil plays a very important part, for if the soil is not well drained, I think that could be the main cause of the trouble. This could apply particularly to a very heavy clay soil, where naturally the drainage is not too good and where the plants are wet and cold during the whole winter. Under these conditions, if the autumn is very wet followed by some severe frosts, it can prove very disastrous. I had an instance of this in the spring of 1957, when certain varieties were badly affected.

I do think that a good covering of old ashes is helpful where the drainage is bad. Over-feeding could also be a cause, as it is so often with dahlias when they are heavily fed to produce large exhibition blooms. In this case the roots are generally rather big and the stems are thick and fleshy. Rotting generally starts at the bottom of the stems and works right down to the base of the tuber, spoiling the entire crown. This is the very part from which cuttings are secured for the next year's plants, and I believe that this disease works in the same way with delphiniums.

Therefore, periodical analysis of the soil should be taken in order to keep the conditions well balanced.

Disease can also be encouraged by dividing delphiniums in the autumn. The plants 'bleed' very badly at times, and this is the wrong period of the year in which to carry out this form of increasing stock, as the sap has not then started its upward flow, nor is it the time when the delphinium makes fresh roots. Therefore one is asking for trouble by making divisions in the autumn.

There is another disease, known as black spot, which attacks certain varieties more than others. You can usually distinguish the disease by the big black spots on the foliage, which eventually dies. Besides the discoloration, it also leads to a good deal of weakening of the plant. That is why it is rather better to propagate from cuttings instead of by division. When I first had training in delphinium growing, all the propagation was carried out by divisions in the spring. There is no doubt that continued propagation by division weakens the plants, with the result that they become very prone to an attack of black spot.

I can honestly say that since going over to rooted cuttings I have seen hardly any disease, whereas previously I had some bad attacks on certain varieties.

As regards pests, slugs seem to revel on delphiniums. Perhaps it is because the roots are especially suitable hiding-places where slug eggs can be concealed. This allows the young slugs to do an immense amount of harm before they are seen. It is therefore a good plan to look over the young plants at frequent intervals, especially during the autumn and winter, and to spray systematically.

There are now numerous good slug destroyers available, and I find that Slugit in pellet or liquid form is most effective. They are made up by the Murphy Chemical Co., Ltd., Wheathampstead, Hertfordshire. Treatment is needed in the late autumn, and very regularly in the spring. Particularly in a wet season, it is quite incredible to see so many dead slugs as a result of using one of these slug killers.

Mildew is liable to occur at any time, even on very young plants raised from seed or cuttings. Fortunately, it is not a disease which is likely to kill the plants, but it makes the foliage and stems most unsightly. It is most likely to appear in late summer, also during cold periods in the spring, some varieties being more susceptible than others. There are various mildew remedies and preventatives on the market, although spraying the plants with green sulphur is both simple and an effective means of dealing with the trouble.

Raisers are now doing their best to breed varieties that are mildew-resistant, as there is nothing so annoying as when this fungus gets a hold of your plants.

⤜ 13 ⤛

Delphinium Species

〜〜〜〜〜〜〜〜〜〜〜〜〜〜〜〜〜

IN THIS BOOK it is impossible to give a complete list of all the known species, so I shall confine myself to a few of the best and most easily obtainable.

I think it is true to say that since gardens are not now so large as in the past, there is not so much demand for the species, chiefly owing to the lack of space.

The public is more interested in the named hybrids, of which there are several hundreds available. However, there are still a few species from which it is hoped to obtain yellow and red delphiniums, although it may be some years before we reach this goal.

After all, it is not very long since the first named white varieties were launched on the market. These were 'Swan Lake', 'Janice' and then 'Everest'. Now we are starting on the pink varieties.

One selection which seems to be causing a certain amount of interest at the Wisley Gardens is the 'West of the Rockies'—a red strain which was originated and introduced by Mr A. A. Samuelson of Pullman, Washington, U.S.A., nearly twenty years ago.

He gathered a collection of species most of which were natives of the western United States. His main objects were to find out their adaptability to garden culture and then to use them in controlled combination, for red development, as a basis for his hybridisation programme. The following were some of the species which were used as parents: *nudicaul, cardinale, menziesii, nelsoni, pairislii, ochroleucum* and *trollifolium.*

The plants raised, which vary in colour, have single florets, varying in size from 1 to 2 inches and are borne on slim but strong stems.

Many of these plants are dwarf in habit, being between 9 inches and 1 foot tall, but there are some which grow to a height of 3 feet or more. In most instances the florets open fully, though the same cannot be said for some of the species from which they originate.

For those who might wish to try their hand at growing them, the following is a list of the better species.

D. *brunonianum* (Himalayas). Purple flowers, hooded like a primulinus gladiolus. Scented in native habitat, but scent is lost when grown in this country.

D. *cardinale* (California). Scarlet florets—needs a light, well-drained soil with full sunshine. It is tuberous rooted. If desired, tuber may be lifted, dried and stored in dry vermiculite during winter months. This is advisable where winter conditions are usually severe.

D. *dictyocarpum* (Siberia). Flowers pale blue, easy to grow and reasonably hardy; has a straight spur.

D. *duhmbergii* (Russia). Blue and white flowers, a robust grower in this country often reaching 6 feet—truly perennial.

D. *nudicaule* (California). Scarlet flowers—florets do not open fully. The variety 'Orange Queen' is probably the best, and seed is often available from well-known seedsmen. Suitable as a pot plant or on a rockery.

D. requienii (S.W. Europe). Flowers are bluish white, with pink and green markings—not a true perennial, but an attractive plant.

D. tatsienense (Szechuan). Showy azure-blue florets, with long spurs. A very graceful flower.

D. triste (Siberia). Florets dark brown, sepals edged with red. Usually performs well in this country.

D. vestitum (Himalayas). Flowers are a deep violet, large spikes, easy to grow and blooms late August.

D. welbyi (Ethiopia). Pale blue flowers—scented in its native habitat. This scent is lost when grown in the open in this country.

D. yunnanensis (China). Flowers bright blue. The colour is good, but form is poor.

D. zalil (Afghanistan). Flowers of medium-yellow tipped with orange spots on two central petals. It is tuberous rooted, needs a well-drained, light soil and full sunshine. It is advisable to lift and store tuber in dry vermiculite during winter.

It is probable that the species *D. zalil* may be the means of producing a Yellow Elatum in the future, and experiments are being carried on at present to try to bring this about. I understand that experiments are also being carried out to bring about a Red Elatum; hence my remarks that were made in a previous chapter of the possibility of covering all the shades in the larkspur. Some experiments are also being carried out to bring scent into the delphinium, so the future may have a lot in store for us.

☙ 14 ☙

The Delphinium Society

〰〰〰〰〰〰〰〰〰〰〰〰〰〰〰〰〰〰

I CONSIDER that no book on delphiniums would be complete without reference to the National Society. This Society was formed in 1928, when it was known as the British Delphinium Society. This name was kept until 1957, when it was changed to the Delphinium Society.

It appears that the American Delphinium Society has ceased to function as a body. As a result, the Delphinium Society has been able to recruit many new members from the U.S.A., Canada, South Africa, Australia, New Zealand and other parts of the world.

This has largely come about as a result of a good deal of correspondence plus some very admirable Year Books which have been produced by Mr Ronald Parrett, Mr Montague Lacey and now Mr George Cairncross. There is a very lively Joint Delphinium Committee which consists of an equal number of representatives from the Royal Horticultural Society and the Delphinium Society. This committee examines the new varieties which are sent for their judgement, and if the committee considers any specimen as outstanding, it can be given an award of merit as an exhibition variety and sent to Wisley for trial as a garden plant, or it can be selected for trial for Wisley only and be judged as a garden plant. If a variety fails to receive an award of merit but is selected for trial at Wisley, the exhibitor of course can always put up the variety again at a later date, but it is better policy to wait and see how it succeeds at Wisley. The whole committee would then know its capabilities when it came before them again.

There are times, of course, when the committee may consider that the variety is too similar to an existing one which flowers at the same time. However, when they are tried together at Wisley it may be found that they are both quite distinct, for it is not too easy to carry all the colours in one's mind at once.

The Delphinium Society is most grateful to the Royal Horticultural Society for conducting the trials at its gardens at Wisley, where judging takes place during June and July. A good representative collection of existing varieties is maintained from which it is easier to assess the capabilities of the new varieties in the trial. There are two awards that can be given in the first place, Award of Merit and Highly Commended. After the variety has been in the trial some time, it is possible for one which was previously given a Highly Commended award to be given the higher Award of Merit. Then, after a year or two, if a variety is quite outstanding, it can be given a first-class certificate, which is the highest award possible. This is an achievement that few plants ever attain. The trials are open to the public for inspection on the production of an R.H.S. pass or by paying at the entrance gate to Wisley Gardens.

All the varieties that have previously received awards are named and are grown in clumps of three plants. They grow rather taller at Wisley than in most places, because the soil there is very sandy and a good deal of humus has to be used to hold the moisture, and this, together with the necessary watering, does tend to make the plants grow higher.

The Delphinium Society also runs a very excellent annual show in London, and it is hoped that as the Society continues to grow it will in the future be able to offer sponsored classes at shows in other parts of the country.

The Society has a keen colony at Leeds, which has been fostered by one or two members in the area, Mr H. S. Wainwright in particular. Mr Wainwright has been President of the Leeds (Roundhay) Summer Show for some years and his wonderful exhibits of delphiniums were always one of the joys of that show. His garden is opened to the public in aid of the National Garden Scheme, and delphiniums have been one of the main features for many years.

A most excellent Year Book is issued by the Delphinium Society annually, besides many other booklets on delphinium culture. A very useful advisory service is in operation for members who have queries or require information.

A very capable Social Committee organises various meetings where the members can discuss their problems, while an excellent annual outing is arranged to one of the leading specialist growers or to the gardens of one or two amateur growers. Finally, during October a very excellent Annual Dinner is held to round off the year's work. All these facilities, most of which are provided voluntarily, make it well worth being a member for the fee of 10s 6d per annum. The present Secretary is Dr C. J. H. Topping, B.A., Ph.D., 5 Park Lane, Sevenoaks, Kent, who will gladly give any other information desired.

⤜ 15 ⤛

Diary for the Year's Work

∽∽∽∽∽∽∽∽∽∽∽∽∽∽∽∽∽∽∽∽∽∽∽∽∽∽∽∽∽

JANUARY

See that your plants in the border are well protected against slugs.

Give plants a good watering of Murphy's 'Slugit' about twice a month.

See that plants are still well protected with ashes to assist with winter drainage.

FEBRUARY

Remove ashes towards the middle or end of month, according to existing weather conditions.

Lift plants for division and divide as instructed.

Lift plants for cuttings and place in cool greenhouse or cold frame.

Keep winter watering programme going to combat slugs.

Sow seed in heated greenhouse, using John Innes Seed Compost.

Prepare your soil and use John Innes No. 1 Compost when seedlings are big enough to handle. The same preparation is required for cuttings when rooted.

Plant out any new plants purchased from nurseries for spring planting.

MARCH

Take your cuttings as soon as ready.

Remember to see that each cutting has a solid base.

Shade from sun until rooted.

Sow seed in unheated greenhouse.

Remember to cover seed very lightly, or germination will fail.

Remove any thin or surplus shoots from plants in your border.

Leave three shoots on 1-year plants, six to eight shoots on older plants.

Keep watering with 'Slugit'.

Continue planting out any new plants purchased from nurseries for spring planting.

APRIL

Continue to take cuttings if available.

Prick out seedlings into trays or pot up individually.

Pot up cuttings as soon as rooted and place in cold frame.

Shade against sun and keep close for a few days.

Keep plants in borders well hoed and free from weeds.

Place canes around each plant, ready for the first tie.

Prepare nursery bed for seedlings and cuttings.

MAY

Continue to pot up cuttings as available.

Prick out seedlings.

Plant out seedlings and rooted cuttings into nursery bed.

Feed plants in main border with dried blood as directed.

Keep soil moving with hoe to keep plants clean.

Ring round canes to support plants.

Water plants well if at all dry.

JUNE

For exhibition spikes remove all laterals, except two small ones on each spike.

Keep plants well watered as required.

Feed plants with sulphate of potash as directed.

Keep plants in nursery bed well watered and clear of weeds.

Instead of nursery bed, plants can be potted into 6-inch pots, using John Innes No. 2 Compost.

To prevent mildew, dust with Vitospor M regularly every ten days.

JULY

Remove centre spike when seeding starts, to help laterals.

For second crop, cut down immediately after flowering if there is plenty of basal growth.

Give each plant a general feed as directed.

Keep well watered and dust against mildew as directed.

Select plants for seed if required.

AUGUST

Plants required for second crop should be re-staked and all laterals removed.

Keep plants well watered if weather is hot and dry.

Seed should be harvested when ready.

Prepare ground for the plants raised in the spring.

SEPTEMBER

Plant out all plants raised in the spring into their flowering quarters.

Cut down all plants from which seed has been saved.

Feed and water well, in order to build up a crown for next season.

Clean round all plants to prevent slugs from hibernating.

OCTOBER

Continue to plant out any plants raised in the spring or purchased from nurseries at summer shows.

Keep plants well hoed and cleaned.

NOVEMBER

Continue to plant out up to middle of month, according to weather conditions.

Cut down all plants that have flowered and clean over carefully.

Give plants a watering of 'Slugit' to kill any slugs.

DECEMBER

Cover the crowns of the plants with ashes to assist winter drainage.

Remove any further decayed foliage.

Fork round the plants carefully.

Give a further watering of 'Slugit' to prevent slug damage.

INDEX